Pyschometric Tests

Numerical

Test 1

MD *Publishing*

Instructions:

In this test you will be presented with a series of graphs, tables and pie charts. For each there will be four multiple choice questions. You must select the appropriate answer in the time given.

Select your answer according to the rules given below:

- each question has only one right answer;

- Rely solely on the information contained within the questions. These tests do no assume any prior knowledge;

- The test should be completed within 30 mins;

- There is no negative marking for incorrect answers;

- You may use a calculator.

Table 1: PC Limited (financial results)

	£'000 2006	£'000 2005
Sales	52,500	47,000
Cost of Sales	(35,610)	(34,000)
Gross Profit	17,890	13,000
Administrative Expenses	(8,640)	(7,520)
Total Profit	9,250	5,480

1) If administrative expenses continue to rise at the same percentage as from 2005 to 2006, what will they be in 2007? *(to the nearest £'000)*

A. 9,927 ____
B. 9,760 ____
C. 7,520 ____
D. 9,867 ____
E. Cannot say ____

Working Pad

2) If sales in the computer industry are expected to rise by 20% from 2006 to 2007, what will the expected sales figure for PC Limited be in 2007? *(to the nearest £'000)*

A. 58,644 ____
B. 63,000 ____
C. 52,500 ____
D. 61,500 ____
E. Cannot say ____

Working Pad

3) What is the percentage increase between 2005 and 2006 for the gross profit margin?
   (Gross profit margin is calculated as: Gross profit / Sales)

   A. 34.07% ____
   B. 23.20% ____
   C. 26.66% ____
   D. 9.41% ____
   E. Cannot say ____

   Working Pad

4) The total industry sector in which PC Limited operate in has a total sales figure for 2006 of £191.8m. In 2006, what is PC Limited's market share of this market based on total sales?

   A. 34.53% ____
   B. 23.20% ____
   C. 27.37% ____
   D. 18.20% ____
   E. Cannot say ____

   Working Pad

   Extra Working Pad

Table 2: Robert Werth LLP (recruitment sources)

	CV's	Press Advertising	Career Fairs	Recruitment Websites	Company Website
2004	9,500	24,500	14,000	8,000	12,000
2005	10,000	21,000	9,500	17,500	21,500
2006	11,500	17,000	7,500	27,000	32,000

The above table presents the number of applicants applying for jobs via different recruitment sources at Robert Werth LLP

5) If offline recruitment sources (CV's, Press Advertising and Career Fairs) cost Robert Werth LLP 20x more per applicant than online recruitment sources (Recruitment Websites and Company Website) per applicant, what was the percentage decrease in the cost of sourcing applicants between 2004 and 2006?

A. 20.51% ____
B. 23.43% ____
C. 10.87% ____
D. 15.16% ____
E. Cannot say ____

Working Pad

6) In 2003 out of the 29,750 applications from press advertising, 2,697 of these were offered jobs with 2,141 eventually accepting the position. If this offer and acceptance rate continues, how many people were employed by Robert Werth LLP in 2005 from press advertising?

A. 1,511 ____
B. 1,617 ____
C. 1,796 ____
D. 849 ____
E. Cannot say ____

Working Pad

Progress Bar

7) In 2004 the cost to Robert Werth of running 7 careers fairs was £24,500. In 2005 the cost of running 5 careers fairs was £19,000 and in 2006 the cost was £14,000 to run 4 careers fairs. In which year did Robert Werth receive the most applicants per £ spent on careers fairs?

A. 2004 ____
B. 2005 ____
C. 2006 ____
D. 2007 ____
E. Cannot say ____

Working Pad

8) What is the percentage increase in the percentage of applicants who applied for jobs with Robert Werth LLP via CVs and recruitment websites between 2005 and 2006?

A. 21.38% ____
B. 19.61% ____
C. 17.17% ____
D. 5.46% ____
E. Cannot say ____

Working Pad

Extra Working Pad

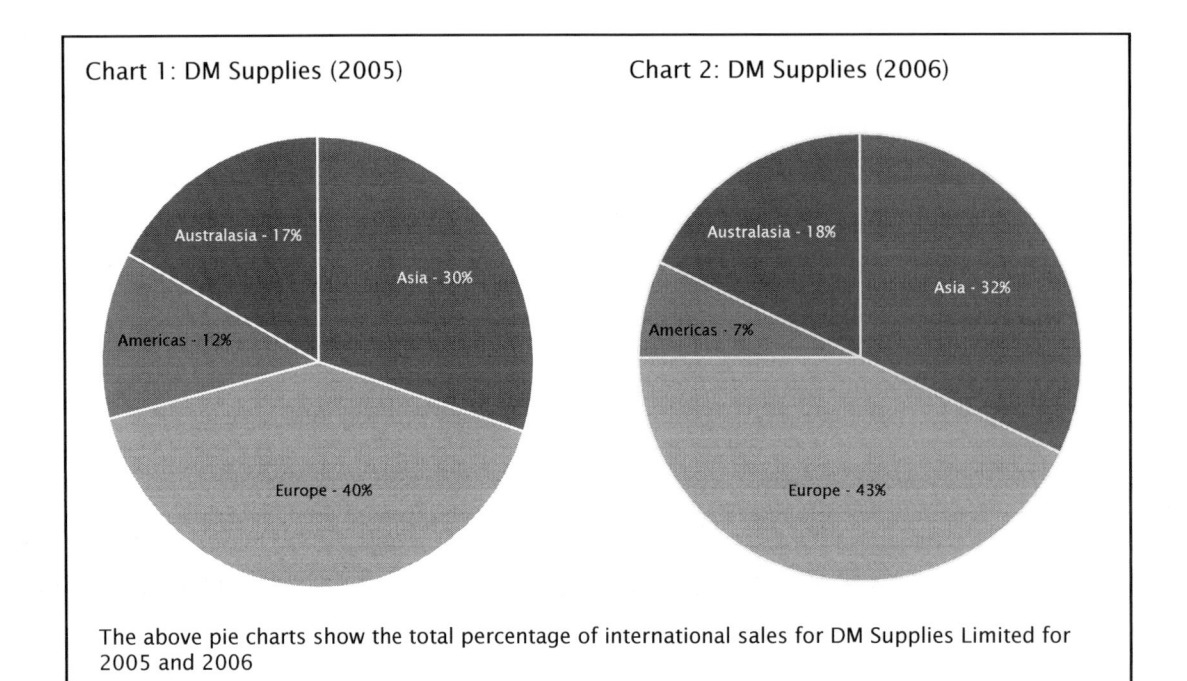

Chart 1: DM Supplies (2005)
- Australasia - 17%
- Asia - 30%
- Americas - 12%
- Europe - 40%

Chart 2: DM Supplies (2006)
- Australasia - 18%
- Asia - 32%
- Americas - 7%
- Europe - 43%

The above pie charts show the total percentage of international sales for DM Supplies Limited for 2005 and 2006

9) Which continent represented the greatest percentage increase in sales between 2005 and 2006?

A. Asia _____
B. Europe _____
C. Americas _____
D. Australasia _____
E. Cannot say _____

Working Pad

10) In 2005 sales in Asia totalled 541,639 units. If total unit sales for DM Supplies Ltd increased by 9% between 2005 and 2006, what was the number of sales in Europe in 2006?

A. 590,387
B. 776,349
C. 740,240
D. 846,221
E. Cannot say

Working Pad

11) The expected sales mix in 2007 suggests that half of DM Supplies Ltd's total sales will be in Asia, Australasia and Americas in the proportions 3:2:1 respectively. If total unit sales are budgeted to be 1.9m in 2007, what amount of sales will Australasia have?

A. 456,333
B. 316,667
C. 633,333
D. 516,000
E. Cannot say

Working Pad

12) Sales in 2005 rose by 8.6% from 2004. What was the number of units sold in Americas in 2004? *(to the nearest unit)*

A. 216,656
B. 199,499
C. 204,767
D. 326,748
E. Cannot say

Working Pad

Table 3: Smiths LLP (2005)

	Audit	Transaction Services (TS)	Corporate Finance (CF)	Taxation
Revenue (£'000)	512	274	267	394
GEI (£'000)	307	196	184	201
Number of Partners	34	21	23	21
Number of Employees	819	707	705	769
Number of Clients	106	34	29	76

13) Which department produced the best GEI per employee during 2005?

A. Audit ____
B. TS ____
C. Tax ____
D. CF ____
E. Cannot Say ____

Working Pad

14) In which two departments did clients have to pay the largest average fees for the service provided?

A. Audit & TS ____
B. Audit & Tax ____
C. TS & CF ____
D. CF & Tax ____
E. Cannot Say ____

Working Pad

15) All departmental partners are remunerated in the same way which is via a profit sharing scheme based on the departments GEI per annum. In 2005 which department's partners received the largest remuneration?

A. Audit ____
B. TS ____
C. Tax ____
D. CF ____
E. Cannot Say ____

Working Pad

16) What was the average remuneration per partner within the Tax department?

A. £94,600 ____
B. £18,762 ____
C. £9,000 ____
D. £9,570 ____
E. Cannot Say ____

Working Pad

Extra Working Pad

Table 4: Picture Limited (revenue per department in £'s)

	Department				
	A	B	C	D	E
January	20	64	10	12	176
February	30	64	6	14	194
March	32	69	9	16	197
April	36	76	17	17	184
May	36	87	18	18	176
June (expected)	36	94	19	20	152

17) Which two departments had the same percentage increase in revenue between January and May?

A. A & B _____
B. B & C _____
C. C & A _____
D. D & B _____
E. A & D _____

Working Pad

18) What was the total revenue produced by all departments in April and May?

A. £360 _____
B. £665 _____
C. £670 _____
D. £756 _____
E. Cannot Say _____

Working Pad

19) In June department A discontinued it's operations due to a cost cutting exercise by Head Office. If department A's expected revenue in June was distributed among departments B, C and D with department D benefitting by twice as much as the other two departments, what would be the total difference between department D's revenue and department B's expected revenue for the 6 months ending in June?

A. £65 ____
B. £312 ____
C. £348 ____
D. £357 ____
E. Cannot Say ____

Working Pad

20) Department B had the option of investing £10,000 in new machinery on 1 February. It was expected that revenue would have increased by 6% per month, two months after purchase of the machine. However Pictures Limited did not have enough cash resources available to purchase the machine on this date.

If the new machine was purchased on 1 February, what would have been the total revenue from this department for the 5 month period from January to May? (to the nearest £).

A. £370 ____
B. £360 ____
C. £382 ____
D. £374 ____
E. £454 ____

Working Pad

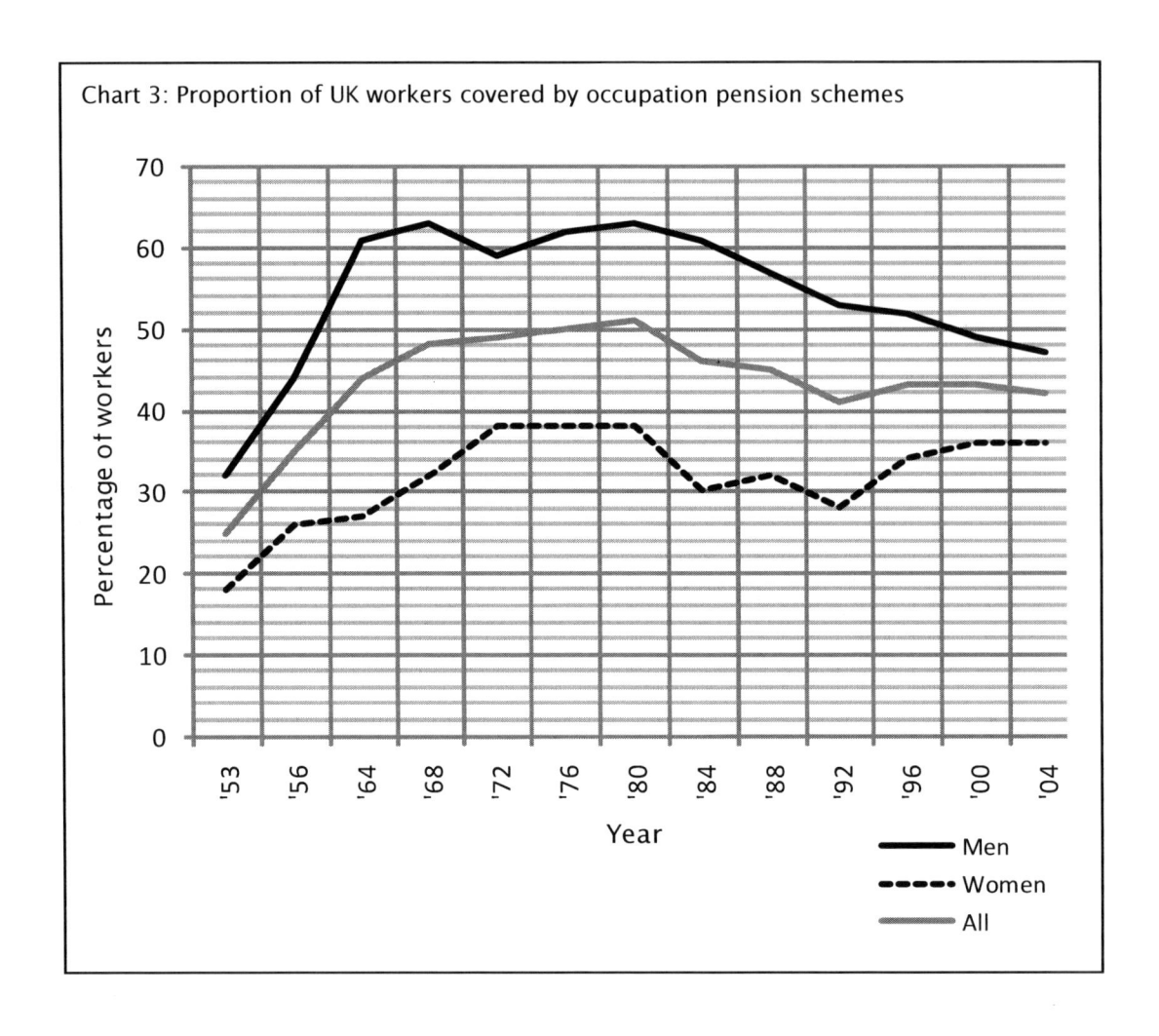

Chart 3: Proportion of UK workers covered by occupation pension schemes

(Line chart showing percentage of workers from '53 to '04 for Men, Women, and All)

21) In 1976, the total amount within the UK occupational pension schemes was £1,674,342,000 with the average female contributing £2,746 per annum and the average male contributing £3,861 per annum.

If the total amount within the occupational pension funds rose 5% over the next 4 years, how much of the pension fund in 1980 related to female contributions? (to the nearest percent)

A. 27% ____
B. 29% ____
C. 32% ____
D. 34% ____
E. Cannot Say ____

Working Pad

22) What was the percentage decrease between the years 1968 and 1984 of the percentage of UK workers who belonged to an occupational pension scheme? (to the nearest percent)

A. 8% ____
B. 4% ____
C. 2% ____
D. 10% ____
E. Cannot Say ____

Working Pad

23) If the average number of men subscribed to an occupational pension scheme continued to decrease at the same rate per annum as between '00 and '04, what would be the average percentage of men subscribed to an occupational pension scheme in 2008?

A. 45% ____
B. 35% ____
C. 24% ____
D. 51% ____
E. Cannot Say ____

Working Pad

24) In what year was the largest difference between the percentage of men and the percentage of women covered by the occupational pension schemes?

A. 2000 ____
B. 1992 ____
C. 1964 ____
D. 1984 ____
E. 1972 ____

Working Pad

Pyschometric Tests

Numerical

Test 2

Numerical - Test 2

MD *Publishing*

Instructions:

In this test you will be presented with a series of graphs, tables and pie charts. For each there will be four multiple choice questions. You must select the appropriate answer in the time given.

Select your answer according to the rules given below:

- each question has only one right answer;

- Rely solely on the information contained within the questions. These tests do no assume any prior knowledge;

- The test should be completed within 30 mins;

- There is no negative marking for incorrect answers;

- You may use a calculator.

Table 1: Armedia Group Limited

Company	Employees	Turnover per week (£'000)	Turnover as a % of last year (£'000)	Profit (£'000)
A	100	60	75	45
B	150	75	120	36
C	200	100	88	44
D	300	250	80	197
E	600	400	105	205

1) Which company produced the highest turnover per employee? (*assuming the number of employees remained constant during the year*)

A. A ____
B. B ____
C. C ____
D. D ____
E. E ____

Working Pad

2) Which company produced the best profit margin? (*profit margin is calculated as profit/turnover*)

A. A ____
B. B ____
C. C ____
D. D ____
E. E ____

Working Pad

Progress Bar

3) If company E continued to grow as it managed to over the last year, what would the turnover per week be in 11 years times? (*to the nearest £'000*)

A. 987
B. 819
C. 684
D. 1,214
E. 4,200

Working Pad

4) What is the annual difference in turnover per employee between company B and E?

A. £8,667
B. £9,000
C. £9,667
D. £6,667
E. £8,000

Working Pad

Extra Working Pad

Progress Bar

Table 2: Premier Sweets Limited

	£'000 2006	£'000 2005
Revenue	100,200	94,600
Gross Profit *	40,080	39,670
Administrative Expenses	(12,420)	(10,390)
Other Income	700	650
Exceptional Costs	(58)	(94)
Total Profit	28,302	29,836

* Gross Profit is calculated as Revenue less Cost Of Sales

5) What is the percentage increase/decrease in Cost of Sales between 2005 and 2006?

- A. 8.7% Decrease
- B. 8.7% Increase
- C. 9.5% Decrease
- D. 9.5% Increase
- E. Cannot Say

Working Pad

6) If Cost of Sales, Administrative Costs, Other Income and Total Profit continue at the same rates as between 2005 and 2006, what will the Revenue be in 2007? (*to the nearest £'000 - assuming there are no Exceptional Costs in 2007*)

- A. £107,896
- B. £106,739
- C. £99,841
- D. £106,132
- E. £104,696

Working Pad

7) If the percentage difference for Administrative Expenses from 2005 to 2006 had remained the same since incorporation of the company, what were Administrative Expenses in 1999? (*to the nearest £'000*)

- A. £5,698 ____
- B. £7,640 ____
- C. £3,561 ____
- D. £4,264 ____
- E. Cannot Say ____

Working Pad

8) Included within the 2006 Administrative Expenses are £6,520 labour costs. If the labour force were halved in 2006, what would Administrative Expenses have been? (*to the nearest £'000*)

- A. £7,860 ____
- B. £2,950 ____
- C. £5,900 ____
- D. £9,160 ____
- E. Cannot Say ____

Working Pad

Extra Working Pad

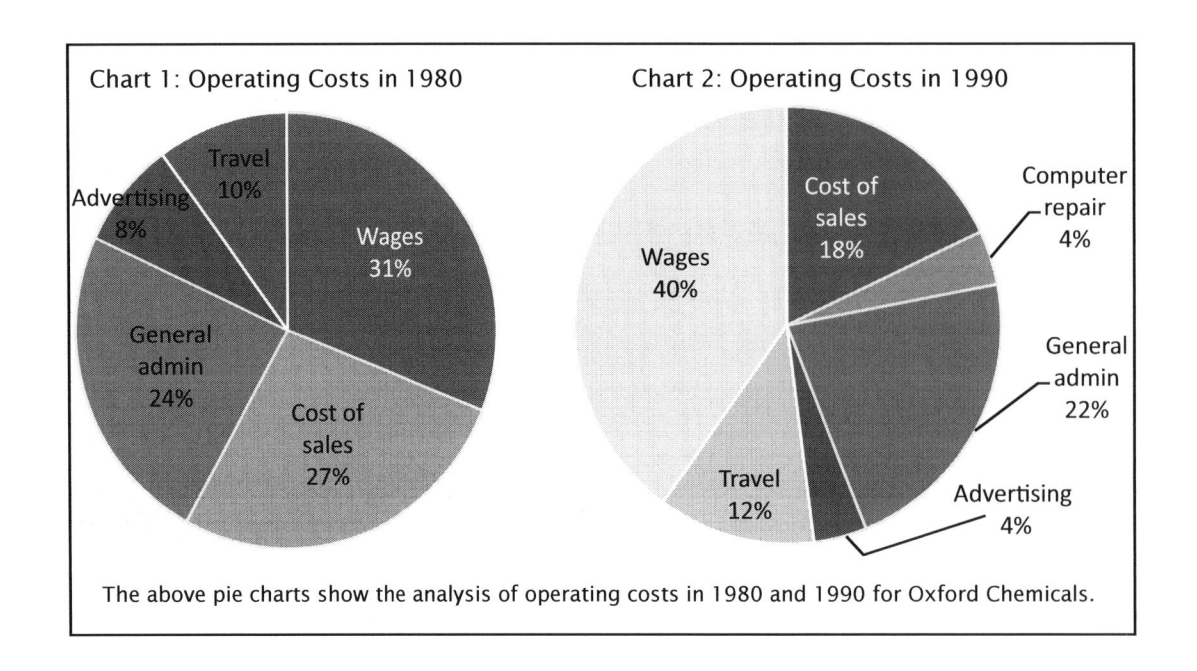

Chart 1: Operating Costs in 1980
- Travel 10%
- Advertising 8%
- General admin 24%
- Cost of sales 27%
- Wages 31%

Chart 2: Operating Costs in 1990
- Cost of sales 18%
- Computer repair 4%
- General admin 22%
- Advertising 4%
- Travel 12%
- Wages 40%

The above pie charts show the analysis of operating costs in 1980 and 1990 for Oxford Chemicals.

9) How much money was spent on advertising in 1990?

A. £4,000 ____
B. £8,000 ____
C. £12,000 ____
D. £16,000 ____
E. Cannot say ____

Working Pad

10) In 1980 total operating costs amounted to £191,840 and over the next 10 years these costs grew by a total of 11.5%. What is the monetary difference between the amount spent on general admin costs in 1980 and general admin costs in 1990?

A. £4,562 ____
B. £1,017 ____
C. £5,295 ____
D. £3,642 ____
E. Cannot say ____

Working Pad

11) Based on total operating costs of £191,840 in 1980 and growing by 11.5% over the next 10 years, what is the real percentage increase in the total wage bill between 1980 and 1990?

A. 9.00% ____
B. 20.50% ____
C. 34.64% ____
D. 43.87% ____
E. Cannot say ____

Working Pad

12) Which of the following statements is an accurate description of the analysis of operating costs for 1980 and 1990? (tick as many as appropriate)

A. Advertising costs have halved between 1980 and 1990 ____
B. Cost of sales, advertising and general admin costs account for over half of the total operating costs in both 1980 and 1990 ____
C. Gross profit has increased in 1990 compared to 1980 ____
D. Economies of scale have helped to reduce Cost of sales ____
E. Labour costs remain the largest cost to the company ____

Working Pad

Table 3: Volume of imports/exports for 1999

	Jan	Feb	Mar	Apr	May	Jun	Total
Imports	110.0	112.4	108.9	114.6	116.7	115.9	678.5
Exports	116.9	117.8	116.7	124.9	128.8	136.9	742.0
Total	226.9	230.2	225.6	239.5	245.5	252.8	1,420.5

13) Between which two months saw the greatest percentage change in imports?

A. Jan - Feb ____
B. Feb - Mar ____
C. Mar - Apr ____
D. Apr - May ____
E. May - Jun ____

Working Pad

14) For the first three months of 1999, what is the approximate ratio of the number of imports to the total imports/exports?

A. 1:3 ____
B. 1:2 ____
C. 2:1 ____
D. 1:4 ____
E. 3:1 ____

Working Pad

15) If the increase in exports is expected to continue at the same rate as from Jan to Jun, what is the estimated number of exports in December 1999?

A. 158.6 ____
B. 160.3 ____
C. 149.4 ____
D. 156.4 ____
E. Cannot Say ____

Working Pad

16) Which of the following results in the largest ratio?

A. Exports in March to Imports in March ____
B. Imports in Jan, Feb and March to Imports in Apr, May and Jun ____
C. Exports to Imports in June ____
D. Imports to Exports in Feb ____
E. Total Imports to total Exports in Mar to Jun ____

Working Pad

Extra Working Pad

Progress Bar

Chart 4: **Historic Gold price (in USD ounces)**

Price of Gold per ounce vs Year (1997–2009)

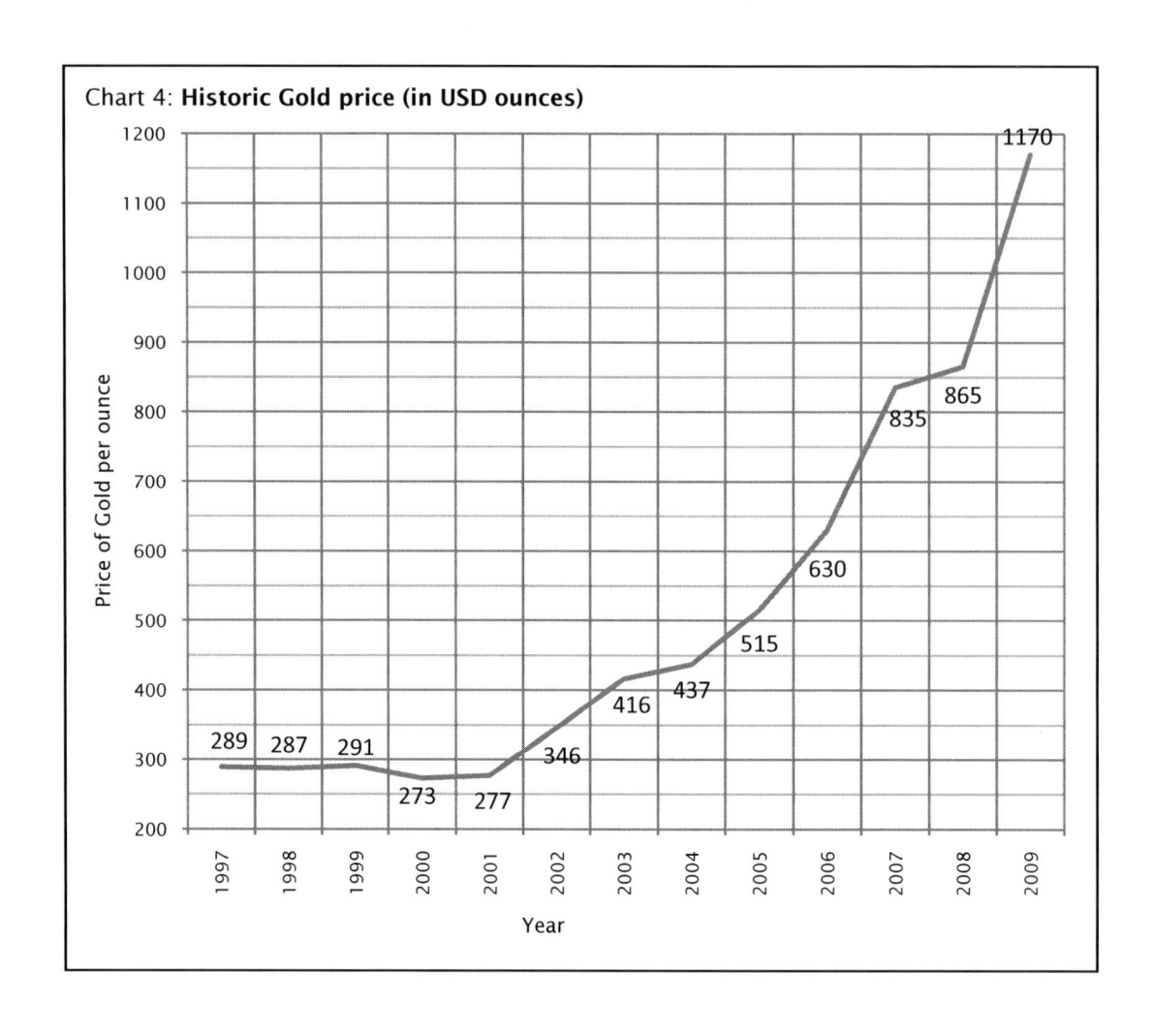

Data points: 1997: 289, 1998: 287, 1999: 291, 2000: 273, 2001: 277, 2002: 346, 2003: 416, 2004: 437, 2005: 515, 2006: 630, 2007: 835, 2008: 865, 2009: 1170

17) If a trader purchased 650 ounces of gold in 2000 and sold them all in 2005, how much money would they have made?

A. $157,300

B. $164,350

C. $334,750

D. $98,750

E. Cannot Say

Working Pad

18) If a UK trader purchased 315 ounces of gold in 2005 when the exchange rate was £1:$1.6 and sold all of them in 2008 when the exchange rate had fallen to £1:$1.45, how much money did the trader make?

A. £68,906 ____
B. £76,034 ____
C. £74,999 ____
D. £86,523 ____
E. Cannot Say ____

Working Pad

19) If a UK trader purchased 50 ounces of gold in 2001 when the exchange rate was $1:£0.67 and sold 1134 grams in 2007 when $1:£0.74, how much profit would they have made on the gold they sold? *(1 ounce =28.35 grams)*

A. £17,292 ____
B. £15,436 ____
C. £13,432 ____
D. £7,985 ____
E. Cannot Say ____

Working Pad

20) Gold is expected to continue to increase over the next 2 years at the rate seen back in 2002-2004. If this happened what would te price of gold be at the end of 2011?

A. $1,478 ____
B. $1,500 ____
C. $1,261 ____
D. $1,548 ____
E. Cannot Say ____

Working Pad

Progress Bar

Chart 5: Population of European country since 1990

Year	Under 16	17-33	34-50	51-67	68 and over
1990	12.1	14.4	11.6	18.9	5.8
1995	13.2	15.1	12.7	23.2	7.9
2000	12.5	14.7	11.4	27.8	11.2
2005	12.6	15.4	11.9	29.4	17.3

Population (in millions)

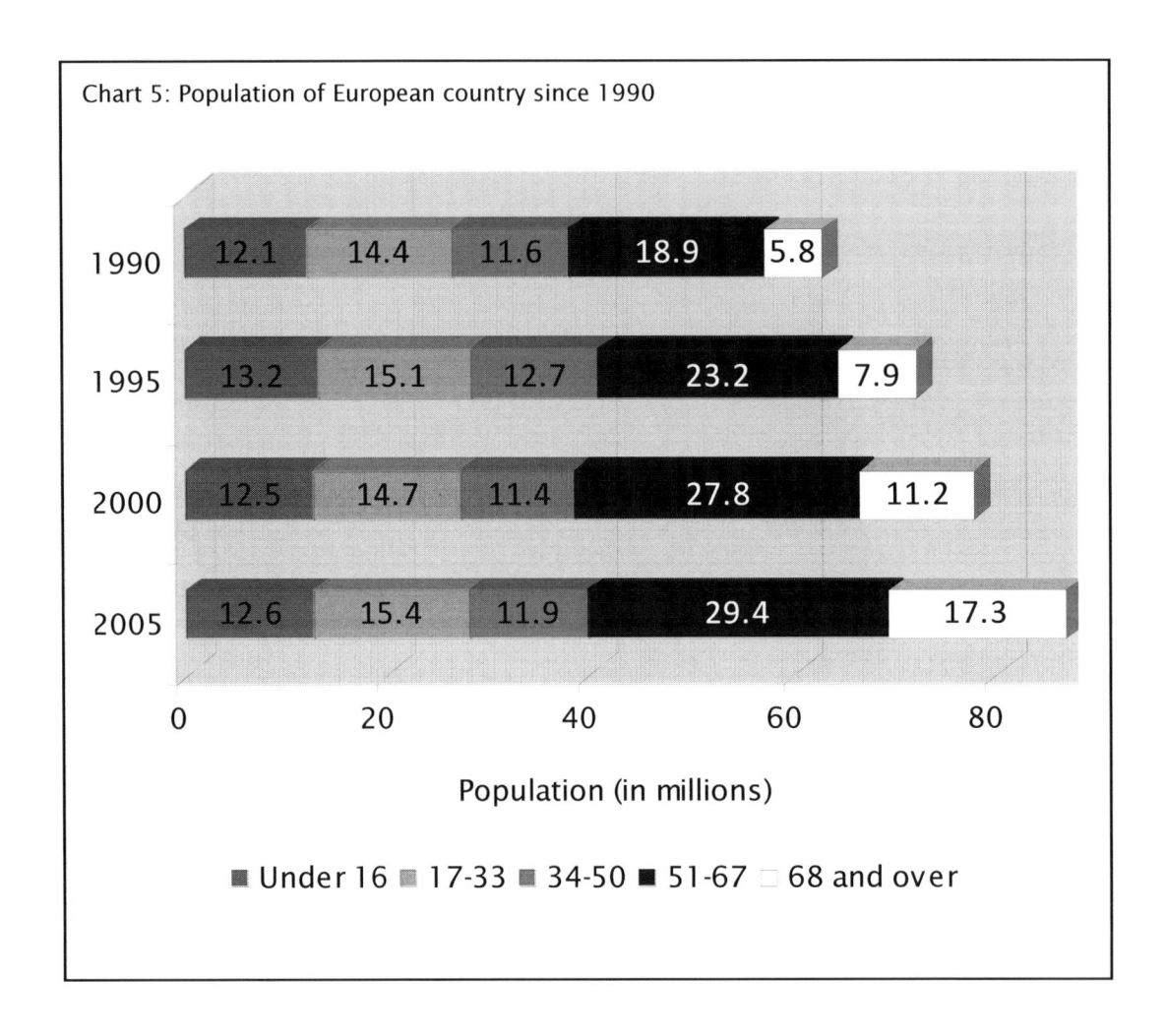

■ Under 16 ■ 17-33 ■ 34-50 ■ 51-67 ☐ 68 and over

21) In 2005 what percentage of the population was aged 51 and over?

A. 53.93%
B. 59.18%
C. 43.67%
D. 47.00%
E. Cannot Say

Working Pad

22) In 2005, 46% of 17-33 year olds were employed. If 6.1 million of those are employed full time, assuming the remainder are working part time how many are employed part time?

A. 2,806,000 ____
B. 617,500 ____
C. 900,000 ____
D. 984,000 ____
E. Cannot Say ____

Working Pad

23) In 1990 how many people were aged between 17 and 50 *(in millions)*?

A. 14.4 ____
B. 11.6 ____
C. 26.0 ____
D. 29.4 ____
E. Cannot Say ____

Working Pad

24) Between which 5 years was the largest percentage change in the number of people aged 16 and younger?

A. 1985 - 1990 ____
B. 1990 - 1995 ____
C. 1995 - 2000 ____
D. 2000 - 2005 ____
E. Cannot Say ____

Working Pad

Progress Bar

Pyschometric Tests

Numerical

Test 3

Numerical - Test 3

MD Publishing

Instructions:

In this test you will be presented with a series of graphs, tables and pie charts. For each there will be four multiple choice questions. You must select the appropriate answer in the time given.

Select your answer according to the rules given below:

- each question has only one right answer;

- Rely solely on the information contained within the questions. These tests do no assume any prior knowledge;

- The test should be completed within 30 mins;

- There is no negative marking for incorrect answers;

- You may use a calculator.

Table 1: Freds Bakery (unit sales per month)

	Month 1	Month 2	Month 3	Month 4	Month 5	Month 6	Total
Brown Bread	790	940	820	1,120	976	1,004	5,650
White Bread	1,269	1,470	969	1,150	1,510	1,490	7,858
Rolls / Other	412	390	364	496	841	691	3,194
Total Sales	2,471	2,800	2,153	2,766	3,327	3,185	16,702

1) In Month 5 and 6, part of the bread mixture became contaminated resulting in below quality bread. This resulted in Freds Bakery having to offer refunds plus a small compensation of £5 per loaf to each customer. This resulted in 45% of white bread sold in Month 6 and 24% in Month 5 requiring a full refund to be paid to customers. If a white loaf of bread is sold for 80p per loaf, how much money has this cost Freds Bakery?

A. £6,412 _____
B. £2,617 _____
C. £4,119 _____
D. £5,991 _____
E. Cannot Say _____

Working Pad

2) Between which two months did brown bread and rolls/other see the largest percentage change in sales?

A. Months 1-2 _____
B. Months 2-3 _____
C. Months 3-4 _____
D. Months 4-5 _____
E. Months 5-6 _____

Working Pad

3) What is the approximate proportion of brown bread sold in Month 3 and Month 5 to Total Sales?

A. 1 : 2 ____
B. 1 : 4 ____
C. 2 : 1 ____
D. 3 : 1 ____
E. 1 : 3 ____

Working Pad

4) If the cost of making one brown loaf is 10p more than a white loaf and if the total costs in Month 4 of making all white loaves was £483, what was the gross profit from brown bread in Month 4, assuming all loaves of bread are sold for 80p? *(Gross profit is calculated as Sales less cost of sales)*

A. £217.00 ____
B. £397.40 ____
C. £313.60 ____
D. £418.00 ____
E. £287.40 ____

Working Pad

Extra Working Pad

Progress Bar

Table 2: Housing Market

	Average Selling Price	Average sale price as a percentage of advertised price	Average time on market for houses and flats (days)	Proportion of houses to flats sold
2004	£121,000	96.0%	41	2.8:1
2005	£137,500	95.0%	34	2.2:1
2006	£155,000	97.0%	27	1.9:1
2007	£180,000	98.5%	21	1.6:1

5) What is the difference in the average advertised price between 2004 and 2007?

A. £61,140
B. £59,900
C. £56,699
D. £59,000
E. Cannot Say

Working Pad

6) If in 2005 the average time a house was on the market was 29 days. How long did the average flat stay on the market in 2005?

A. 39 days
B. 34 days
C. 45 days
D. 13 days
E. Cannot Say

Working Pad

7) If the average listing price is expected to increase by 5% between 2007 and 2008, what is the percentage increase in the average selling price between the two years?

A. 6.5% ____
B. 7.0% ____
C. 5.0% ____
D. 4.9% ____
E. Cannot Say ____

Working Pad

8) If the average selling price of a house in 2006 was £192,500, what was the average listing price of a flat in 2006?

A. £86,340 ____
B. £83,750 ____
C. £101,750 ____
D. £96,740 ____
E. Cannot Say ____

Working Pad

Extra Working Pad

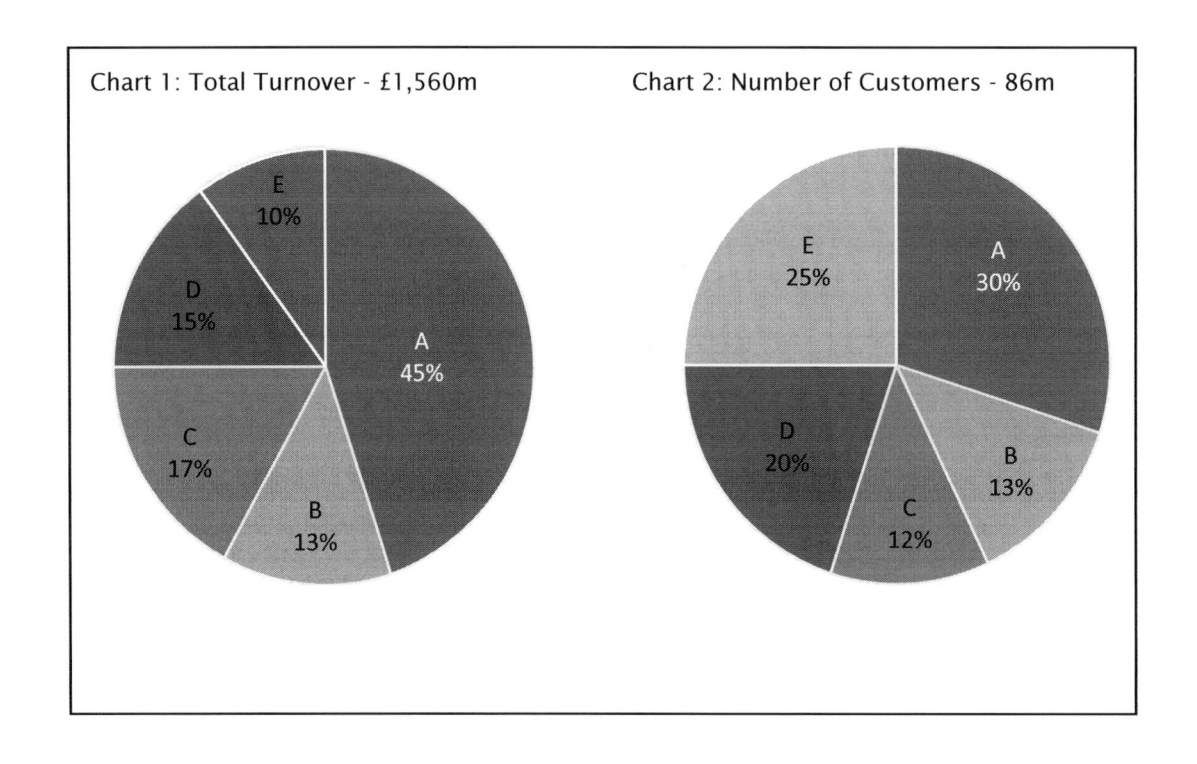

Chart 1: Total Turnover - £1,560m
Chart 2: Number of Customers - 86m

Chart 1:
- A 45%
- B 13%
- C 17%
- D 15%
- E 10%

Chart 2:
- A 30%
- B 13%
- C 12%
- D 20%
- E 25%

9) How many more customers would company B require to generate the same turnover as that of A? *(to the nearest million customers)*

A. 28m ____
B. 26m ____
C. 15m ____
D. 32m ____
E. Cannot say ____

Working Pad

10) If A were to shut all its stores such that the customers went to stores D and E at a ratio of 6:5 how much money would D receive on the assumption that the new customers spend on average the same as the existing customers at D?

   A. £73m   ____
   B. £191m   ____
   C. £208m   ____
   D. £166m   ____
   E. Cannot say ____

   Working Pad

11) If the average spend of customers at C were to increase by £5.60, what level of turnover could they expect?

   A. £265m   ____
   B. £294m   ____
   C. £301m   ____
   D. £323m   ____
   E. Cannot say ____

   Working Pad

12) Which store has the highest average spend per customer?

   A. A ____
   B. B ____
   C. C ____
   D. D ____
   E. E ____

   Working Pad

Chart 3: Total CO2 Emissions

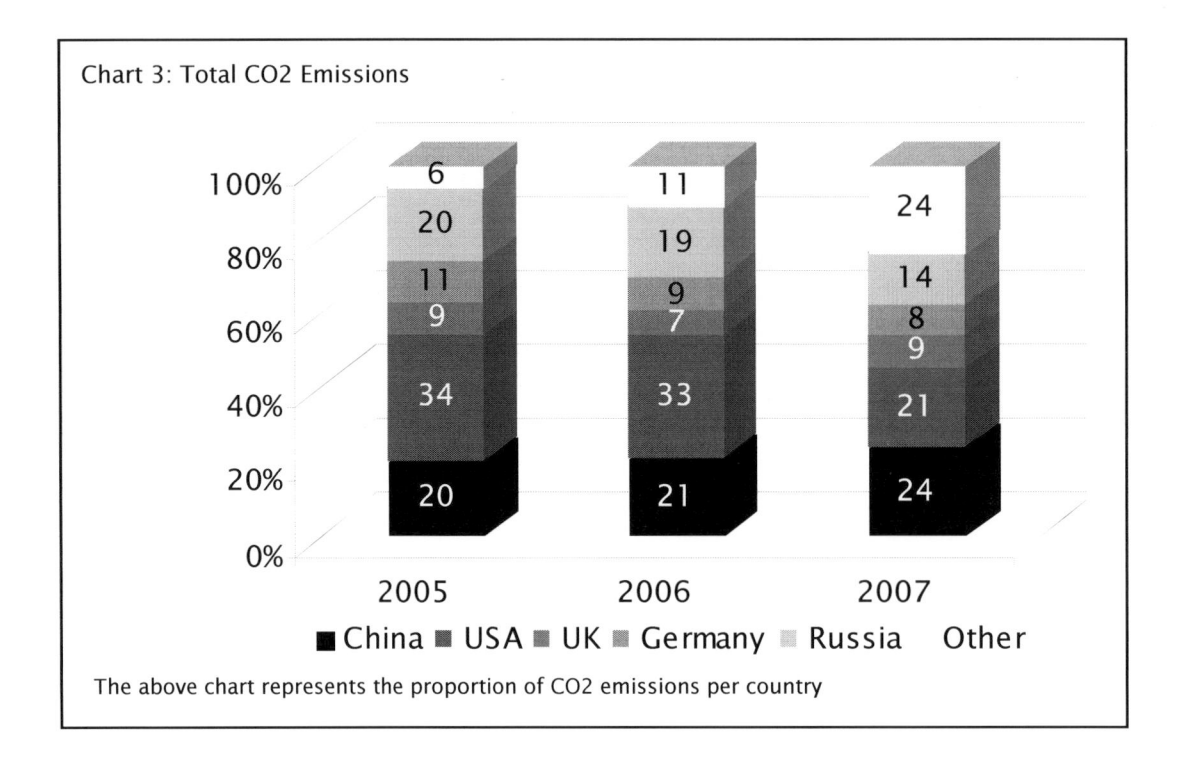

	2005	2006	2007
Other	6	11	24
Russia	20	19	14
Germany	11	9	8
UK	9	7	9
USA	34	33	21
China	20	21	24

■ China ■ USA ■ UK ■ Germany ■ Russia ■ Other

The above chart represents the proportion of CO2 emissions per country

13) If the CO2 emissions worldwide in 2005 were 1.6 billion, what was Germany's contribution to the 2007 CO2 emissions if total emissions increased by 4% p.a. between 2005 and 2007? *(to the nearest million)*

A. 140m
B. 138m
C. 136m
D. 131m
E. Cannot say

Working Pad

14) Between the years 2005 to 2007 inclusive, which country had the largest CO2 emissions?

A. USA ____
B. China ____
C. UK ____
D. Germany ____
E. Russia ____

Working Pad

15) It is expected that global CO2 emissions will decrease by 6.4% by 2010, however due to the increased production in China, it is also expected that China will increase it's CO2 emissions by 4.6% by 2010. What amount of CO2 emissions will the UK have in 2010? *(2005 global emissions were 1.6bn)*

A. 135m ____
B. 112m ____
C. 146m ____
D. 94m ____
E. Cannot say ____

Working Pad

16) Within the UK, factories and offices contribute 68% of the CO2 emissions, cars 27%, houses 4%, and other 1%. If government regulations come into force such that UK factories and offices must cut their emissions by 20% and houses by 2%, with other sources remaining the same what will be the percentage of the emissions of the UK compared with the rest of the world based on 2007 data?

A. 5.4% ____
B. 5.0% ____
C. 6.3% ____
D. 7.8% ____
E. Cannot Say ____

Working Pad

Table 3: Total cars worldwide in 2007

	Number of cars produced (000's)	Number of cars bought by customers	Number of production models
FAIT	1,872	1,273	41
FORDS	3,468	2,019	34
CHEETAH	1,118	827	27
SAB	982	599	21

17) Which car manufacturer had the largest percentage of cars unsold in 2007?

A. FAIT ____
B. FORDS ____
C. CHEETAH ____
D. SAB ____
E. Cannot Say ____

Working Pad

18) CHEETAH's range of cars include the A1, A2, A3, A4 and A5. The A1 accounted for 19% of cars produced by CHEETAH, A2 for 19%, A3 for 26%, A4 for 12% and the A5 for the remaining. If out of the total A5's produced 86% were purchased by customers, how many A5's were sold in 2007? *(in thousands)*

A. 226.91 ____
B. 230.76 ____
C. 204.19 ____
D. 215.38 ____
E. Cannot Say ____

Working Pad

19) FORDS and FAIT target the same customer base along with 7 other car manufacturers around the world. The total number of cars sold to this customer base in 2007 was 11.197 million which is expected to grow by 4% p.a. for the next 7 years. FORDS aims to occupy 44% of this market by 2010. If so, how many more cars each year does FORDS need to sell in order to hit this target assuming the production growth will be the same each year for FORDS?

A. 1.12m ____
B. 1.54m ____
C. 1.69m ____
D. 1.17m ____
E. Cannot Say ____

Working Pad

20) SAB are planning on introducing a new model in 2008 which would increase it's production of all cars to 1.692m. If production of their current models are expected to increase by 4.2% in 2008, how many new model cars will need to be prodcued in 2008? *(to the nearest thousand)*

A. 781 ____
B. 654 ____
C. 720 ____
D. 669 ____
E. Cannot Say ____

Working Pad

Extra Working Pad

Chart 4: Average house prices in Poland

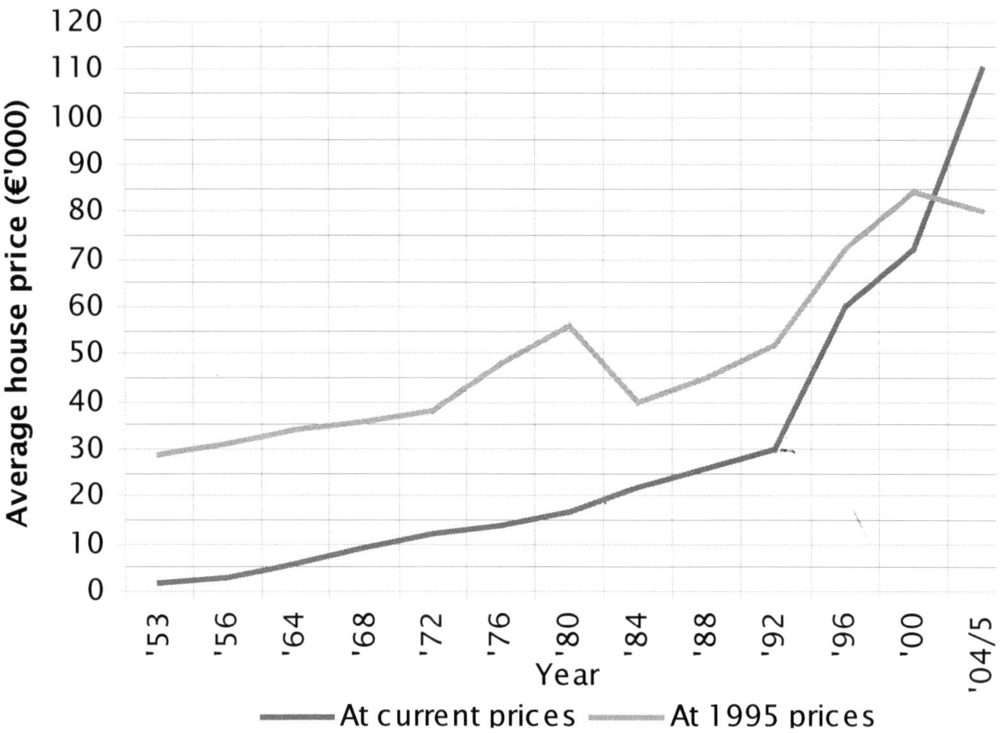

The above chart shows the average EURO house price in Poland at the current prices and also at the constant 1995 value

21) If in 1990, Mr Smith bought a house in Poland for €34,500, how much would the house be worth in 2000?

A. €71k ____

B. €75k ____

C. €51k ____

D. €76k ____

E. Cannot say ____

Working Pad

22) Between which 10 years did the housing market in the Poland perform the best? *(at current prices)*

A. 1980 - 1990 ____
B. 1988 - 1998 ____
C. 1994 - 2004 ____
D. 1976 - 1986 ____
E. Cannot Say ____

Working Pad

23) Mr Smith sold his house in 1992 for the average house price (current prices) and invested the full sale proceeds in a 3% p.a. fixed rate bond. If in 2002 Mr Smith wanted to get back onto the housing market at the average house price, how much additional money would he need to raise in order to afford this? *(to the nearest thousand)*

A. €20,000 ____
B. €24,000 ____
C. €50,000 ____
D. €44,000 ____
E. €36,000 ____

Working Pad

24) If in 1972 a house was purchased for 42% more than the average house price, in which of the following years would that person first see a return on their investment based on average current house prices?

A. 1974 ____
B. 1980 ____
C. 1984 ____
D. 1990 ____
E. Cannot Say ____

Working Pad

Progress Bar

A

Numerical

MD *Publishing*

Pyschometric Tests

Numerical

ANSWER BOOKLETS

Pyschometric Tests

Numerical

Test 1 answers

Question 1: If administrative expenses continue to rise at the same percentage as from 2005 to 2006, what will they be in 2007? (to the nearest £'000).	Answer: A

Working & Answer:

$1 + \dfrac{8,640 - 7,520}{7,520} = 114.89\%$

$114.89\% \times 8,640 = 9,926.809$

Answer

9,927 (A)

Question 2: If sales in the computer industry are expected to rise by 20% from 2006 to 2007, what will the expected sales figure for PC Limited be in 2007? (to the nearest £'000).	Answer: E

Answer:

Although we have been provided with the sales growth for the entire computer industry, this is an average for the industry as a whole and hence cannot be used to calculate the sales for PC Limited. Therefore the answer is:

Cannot Say (E)

Question 3: What is the percentage increase between 2005 and 2006 for the gross profit margin? (Gross profit margin is calculated as: Gross profit / Sales).	Answer: B

Working & Answer:

Gross profit margin in 2005 $= \dfrac{13,000}{47,000} = 27.66\%$

Gross profit margin in 2006 $= \dfrac{17,890}{52,500} = 34.08\%$

Percentage increase between 2005 and 2006 $= \dfrac{34.08\% - 27.66\%}{27.66\%} = 23.1985$

Answer

23.20% (B)

Question 4: The total industry sector in which PC Limited operate in has a total sales figure for 2006 of £191.8m. In 2006, what is PC Limited's market share of this market based on total sales?	Answer: C

Working & Answer:

$\dfrac{52,500}{191,800} = 27.3723$

Answer

27.37% (C)

Question 5: If offline recruitment sources (CV's, Press Advertising and Career Fairs) cost Robert Werth LLP 20x more than online recruitment sources (Recruitment Websites and Company Website) per applicant, what was the percentage decrease in the cost of sourcing applicants between 2004 and 2006?	Answer: A

Working & Answer:

Cost in 2004 = (9,500+24,500+14,000) x 20 + 8,000 + 12,000 = 980,000

Cost in 2006 = (11,500+17,000+7,500) x 20 + 27,000 + 32,000 = 779,000

Percentage increase between 2004 and 2006 = $\frac{779,000 - 980,000}{980,000}$ = -0.2051

<u>Answer</u>

20.51% (A)

Question 6: In 2003 out of the 29,750 applications from press advertising, 2,697 of these were offered jobs with 2,141 eventually accepting the position. If this offer and acceptance rate continues, how many people were employed by Robert Werth LLP in 2005 from press advertising?	Answer: A

Working & Answer:

$\frac{2,141}{29,750}$ = 7.1966%

21,000 x 7.1966% = 1,511

<u>Answer</u>

1,511 (A)

Question 7: If In 2004 the cost to Robert Werth of running 7 careers fairs was £24,500. In 2005 the cost of running 5 careers fairs was £19,000 and in 2006 the cost was £14,000 to run 4 careers fairs. In which year did Robert Werth receive the most applicants per £ spent on careers fairs?	Answer: A

Working & Answer:

2004 = $\frac{24,500}{14,000}$ = £1.75 per applicant

2005 = $\frac{19,000}{9,500}$ = £2.00 per applicant

2006 = $\frac{14,000}{7,500}$ = £1.87 per applicant

<u>Answer</u>

2004 (A)

Question 8: What is the percentage increase in the percentage of applicants who applied for jobs with Robert Werth LLP via CVs and recruitment websites between 2005 and 2006?	Answer: **C**

Working & Answer:

Percentage of applicants in 2005 = $\dfrac{(10,000 + 17,500)}{10,000+21,000+9,500+17,500+21,500}$

= 0.3459

Percentage of applicants in 2006 = $\dfrac{(11,500 + 27,000)}{11,500+17,000+7,500+27,000+32,000}$

= 0.4053

Percentage increase between 2005 and 2006 = $\dfrac{40.53\% - 34.59\%}{34.59\%}$ = 17.17%

<u>Answer</u>

17.17% (C)

Question 9: Which continent represented the greatest percentage increase in sales between 2005 and 2006?	Answer: **E**

Working & Answer:

Although we have been provided with the sales percentage by region, we have not been provided with the absolute sales numbers for 2005 or 2006 and therefore it is not possible to calculate which continent had the greatest percentage increase in sales. Therefore the answer is:

Cannot Say (E)

Question 10: In 2005 sales in Asia totalled 541,639. If total sales for DM Supplies Ltd increased by 9% between 2005 and 2006, what was the number of sales in Europe in 2006?	Answer: **D**

Working & Answer:

Total sales for DM Supplies in 2005 = $\dfrac{541,639}{0.3}$ = 1,805,463

Total sales for DM Supplies in 2006 = 1,805,463 x 1.09 = 1,967,955

Total sales in Europe in 2006 = 1,967,955 x 43%
= 846,220.66

<u>Answer</u>

846,221 (D)

Question 11: The expected sales mix in 2007 suggests that half of DM Supplies Ltd's total sales will be in Asia, Australasia and Americas in the proportions 3:2:1 respectively. If total sales are budgeted to be 1.9m in 2007, what amount of sales will Australasia have?	Answer: **B**

Working & Answer:

Total sales in Asia, Australasia and Americas = $\underline{1,900,000}$ = 950,000
2

Total sales in Australasia = $\underline{950,000 \times 2}$ = 316,666.67
6

<u>Answer</u>

316,667 (B)

Question 12: Sales in 2005 rose by 8.6% from 2004. What was the number of units sold in Americas in 2004? (to the nearest unit).	Answer: **E**

Answer:

The question does not provide the percentage split per region for DM Supplies Limited for 2004, nor the total sales for DM Supplies. Hence it is not possible to calculate the sales in Americas. You cannot assume the sales percentage by region in 2005 were the same in 2004.

Cannot Say (E)

Question 13: Which department produced the best GEI per employee during 2005?	Answer: **A**

Working & Answer:

GEI per employee for Audit = $\underline{307}$ = 0.3748
819

GEI per employee for TS = $\underline{196}$ = 0.2772
707

GEI per employee for CF = $\underline{184}$ = 0.2610
705

GEI per employee for Taxation = $\underline{201}$ = 0.2614
769

<u>Answer</u>

Audit (A)

Question 14: In which two departments did clients have to pay the largest average fees for the service provided?	Answer: **C**

Working & Answer:

Fees per department per client: Audit = $\underline{512}$ = 4.8302
106

Fees per department per client: TS = $\frac{274}{34}$ = 8.059

Fees per department per client: CF = $\frac{267}{29}$ = 9.207

Fees per department per client: Taxation = $\frac{394}{76}$ = 5.1842

<u>Answer</u>

TS & CF (C)

Question 15: All departmental partners are remunerated in the same way which is via a profit sharing scheme based on the departments GEI per annum. In 2005 which department's partners received the largest remuneration?	Answer: C

Working & Answer:

Partners remuneration: Audit = $\frac{307}{34}$ = 9.029

Partners remuneration: TS = $\frac{196}{21}$ = 9.333

Partners remuneration: CF = $\frac{184}{23}$ = 8.000

Partners remuneration: Taxation = $\frac{201}{21}$ = 9.5714

<u>Answer</u>

Tax (C)

Question 16: What was the average remuneration per partner within the Tax department?	Answer: E

Answer:

Although in question 15 you were provided information on how partners were remunerated within Smiths LLP, no information was not provided in question 16 or the original question table. As such with the information provided in question 16 it is not possible to determine the average remuneration per tax partner.

Cannot Say (E)

Question 17: Which two departments had the same percentage increase in revenue between January and May?	Answer: C

Working & Answer:

Department A increase in sales = $\frac{36 - 20}{20}$ = 80.00%

Department B increase in sales = $\frac{87 - 64}{64}$ = 35.94%

Department C increase in sales = $\frac{18 - 10}{10}$ = 80.00%

Department D increase in sales = $\frac{18 - 12}{12}$ = 50.00%

Department E increase in sales = $\frac{176 - 176}{176}$ = 0.00%

<u>Answer</u>

C & A (C)

Question 18: What was the total revenue produced by all departments in April and May?	Answer: **B**

Working & Answer:

Total revenue = 36 + 76 + 17 + 17 + 184 + 36 + 87 + 18 + 18 + 176 = 665

<u>Answer</u>

665 (B)

Question 19: In June department A discontinued it's operations due to a cost cutting exercise by Head Office. If department A's expected revenue in June was distributed among departments B, C and D with department D benefitting by twice as much as the other two departments, what would be the total difference between department D's revenue and department B's expected revenue for the 6 months ending in June?	Answer: **C**

Working & Answer:

Department A closure would provide additional revenue as follows:

Department D = $\frac{36}{2}$ = 18

Department B = $\frac{36}{4}$ = 9

Department C = $\frac{36}{4}$ = 9

As such, Department D's total revenue for the 6 months ending in June would be = 12 + 14 + 16 + 17 + 18 + 20 + 18 (additional revenue) = 115

Department B's total revenue for the 6 months ending in June would be
= 64 + 64 + 69 + 76 + 87 + 94 + 9 (additional revenue) = 463

Therefore the total difference between Department B and Department D is
= 463 - 115 = 348

<u>Answer</u>

£348 (C)

Question 20: Department B had the option if investing £10,000 in new machinery on 1 February. It was expected that revenue would have increased by 6% per month, two months after purchase of the machine. However Pictures Limited did not have enough cash resources available to purchase the machine on this date. If the new machine was purchased on 1 February, what would have been the total revenue from this department for the 5 month period from January to May? (to the nearest £).	Answer: **A**

Working & Answer:

If Department B invested in the machine, revenue would have been as follows:

= 64 + 64 + 69 + (76 x 1.06) + (87 x 1.06) = 369.78

<u>Answer</u>

£370 (A)

Question 21: In 1976, the total amount within the UK occupational pension schemes was £1,674,342,000 with the average female contributing £2,746 per annum and the average male contributing £3,861 per annum. If the total amount within the occupational pension funds rose 5% over the next 4 years, how much of the pension fund in 1980 related to female contributions? (to the nearest percent)	Answer: **E**

Answer:

Although the question provides the female and male pension contributions in 1976, this information is not provided for 1980 and hence this question cannot be answered. You cannot assume the contributions per person in 1976 were the same in 1980.

Cannot Say (E)

Question 22: What was the percentage decrease between the years 1968 and 1984 of the percentage of UK workers who belonged to an occupational pension scheme? (to the nearest percent)	Answer: **C**

Working & Answer:

$$= \frac{46\% - 48\%}{46\%}$$

= -4.2%

<u>Answer</u>

4% (B)

| Question 23: If the average number of men subscribed to an occupational pension scheme continued to decrease at the same rate per annum as between '00 and '04, what would be the average percentage of men subscribed to an occupational pension scheme in 2008? | Answer: **A** |

Working & Answer:

Percentage decrease between '00 and '04 = $\frac{49\% - 47\%}{49\%}$ *= -4.08%*

Therefore estimated number of men in 2008 = 47 × $\frac{(100 - 4.08)}{100}$ *= 45.12*

<u>Answer</u>

45% (A)

| Question 24: In what year was the largest difference between the percentage of men and the percentage of women covered by the occupational pension schemes? | Answer: **C** |

Working & Answer:

TIP: By simply looking at the chart presented in this question, it is clear that the largest differences are in years 1964, 1968, 1980, 1984, 1988 and 1992.

1964 = Men 61 – Women 27 = 34% difference

1968 = Men 63 – Women 32 = 31% difference

1980 = Men 63 – Women 38 = 25% difference

1984 = Men 61 – Women 30 = 31% difference

1988 = Men 57 – Women 32 = 25% difference

1992 = Men 53 – Women 28 = 25% difference

<u>Answer</u>

1964 (C)

Pyschometric Tests

Numerical

Test 2 answers

Question 1: Which company produced the highest turnover per employee? (assuming the number of employees remained constant during the year)	Answer: D

Working & Answer:

Company A = 60 / 100 = 0.6

Company B = 75 / 150 = 0.5

Company C = 100 / 200 = 0.5

Company D = 250 / 300 = 0.83

Company E = 400 / 600 = 0.67

Answer

Company D (D)

TIP: Although the turnover provided within the question is per week, there is no need to multiply each company's revenue by 52 weeks (in order to show the turnover per employee per annum) in order to work out the correct answer.

Question 2: Which company produced the best profit margin? (profit margin is calculated as profit/turnover)	Answer: D

Working & Answer:

Company A = 45 / 60 = 75%

Company B = 36 / 75 = 48%

Company C = 44 / 100 = 44%

Company D = 197 / 250 = 78.8%

Company E = 205 / 400 = 51.25%

Answer

Company D (D)

Question 3: If company E continued to grow as it managed to over the last year, what would the turnover per week be in 11 years times? (to the nearest £'000)	Answer: C

Working & Answer:

Turnover per week in 11 years = 400 x (1.05 ^ 11) = 684.14

Answer

684 (C)

Question 4: What is the annual difference in annual turnover per employee between Company B and Company E? (to the nearest £)	Answer: A

Working & Answer:

Company B = (£75,000 x 52 weeks) / 150 employees = £26,000

Company E = (£400,000 x 52 weeks) / 600 employees = £34,666.67

Difference between Company B and E = £34,666.67 - £26,000 = £8,666.67

Answer

£8,667 (A)

Question 5: What is the percentage increase/decrease in Cost of Sales between 2005 and 2006?	Answer: C

Working & Answer:

2006 Cost of Sales = 100,200 – 40,080 = 60,120

2005 Cost of Sales = 94,600 – 39,670 = 54,930

Percentage difference between 2005 and 2006 = $\frac{60,120 - 54,940}{54,930}$

= 9.45%

Answer

9.5% increase (C)

Question 6: If Cost of Sales, Administrative Costs, Other Income and Total Profit continue at the same rates as between 2005 and 2006, what will the Revenue be in 2007? (assuming there are no Exceptional Costs in 2007)?	Answer: B

Working & Answer:

	2005	2006	Percentage change	2007
Cost of Sales	54,930	60,120	9.45%	65,800
Administrative Costs	(10.390)	(12.420)	19.54%	(14,846)
Other Income	650	700	7.69%	754
Exceptional Costs	(94)	(58)	n/a	0
Total Profit	29,836	28,302	(5.14%)	26,847

Therefore Revenue = 40,939 Gross Profit + 65800 Cost of Sales = 106,739

Answer

106,739 (B)

Question 7: If the percentage difference for Administrative Expenses from 2005 to 2006 had remained the same since incorporation of the company, what were Administrative Expenses in 1999?	Answer: **C**

Working & Answer:

Percentage difference from 2005 to 2006 = (12,420 - 10,390) / 10,390

= 19.538%

Administrative Expenses in 1999 = 10,390 / (1.19538 ^ 6)

= 3,561.06

<u>Answer</u>

3,561 (C)

Question 8: Included within the 2006 Administrative Expenses are £6,520 labour costs. If the labour force were halved in 2006, what would Administrative Expenses have been?	Answer: **E**

Answer:

It is incorrect to assume that all employees are paid the same rates and therefore cutting the number of staff does not necessarily mean cutting the labour costs in half.

Cannot Say (E)

Question 9: How much money was spent on advertising in 1990?	Answer: **E**

Answer:

The question has not provided the total operating costs and therefore this question cannot be answered.

Cannot Say (E)

Question 10: In 1980 total operating costs amounted to £191,840 and over the next 10 years these costs grew by a total of 11.5%. What is the monetary difference between the amount spent on general admin costs in 1980 and general admin costs in 1990?	Answer: **B**

Working & Answer:

General admin costs in 1980 = £191,840 x 24% = £46,041.60

General admin costs in 1990 = £191,840 x 1.115 x 22% = £47,058.35

Monetary difference = £47,058.35 - £46,041.60 = £1,016.75

<u>Answer</u>

£1,017 (B)

Question 11: Based on total operating costs of £191,840 in 1980 and growing by 11.5% over the next 10 years, what is the real percentage increase in the total wage bill between 1980 and 1990?	Answer: **D**

Working & Answer:

Wage costs in 1980 = £191,840 x 31% = £59,470.40

Wage costs in 1990 = £191,840 x 1.115 x 40% = £85,560.64

Percentage increase = $\frac{£85,560.64 - £59,470.40}{£59,470.40}$ = 43.87%

<u>Answer</u>

43.87% (D)

Question 12: Which of the following statements is an accurate description of the analysis of operating costs for 1980 and 1990? (tick as many as appropriate)?	Answer: **E**

Answer:

A. "Advertising costs have halved between 1980 and 1990" – Cannot say as although the percentage has halved from 8% to 4% of total operating costs the actual costs may not have. For example:

	1980	1990 (say)
Total costs	191,840	213,920
Advertising costs at 8%	15,347	
Advertising costs at 4%		8,556
The percentage difference using the above example is therefore 44% and not 50%		

B. "Cost of sales, advertising and general admin costs account for over half of the total operating costs in both 1980 and 1990" – This is incorrect as although cost of sales, advertising and general admin costs account for 59% of total operating costs in 1980, these costs only account for 44% of total operating costs in 1990.

C. "Gross profit has increased in 1990 compared to 1980" – Cannot say as the question does not provide the necessary information to calculate gross profit figures.

D. "Economies of scale have helped to reduce Cost of sales" – Cannot say as the question does not provide any explanations for the changes in costs.

E. "Labour costs remain the largest cost to the company" – This is correct

Therefore the answer is that E should be the only option selected. Note that if other options were also selected, no mark will be awarded

Question 13: Between which two months saw the greatest percentage change in imports?	Answer: **C**

Working & Answer:

Jan - Feb = (112.4 – 110.0) / 110.0 = 2.18%

Feb - Mar = (108.9 – 112.4) / 112.4 = (3.11%)

Mar - Apr = (114.6 – 108.9) / 108.9 = 5.23%

Apr - May = (116.7 – 114.6) / 114.6 = 1.83%

May - Jun = (115.9 – 116.7) / 116.7 = (0.69%)

Answer

Mar - Apr (C)

Question 14: For the first three months of 1999, what is the approximate ratio of the number of imports to the total imports and exports?	Answer: **B**

Working & Answer:

Total imports = 110.0 + 112.4 + 108.9 = 331.3

Total imports and exports = 226.9 + 230.2 + 225.6 = 682.7

Ratio = 331.3 : 682.7

The closest and best approximate ration is therefore 1:2

Answer

1:2 (B)

Question 15: If the increase in exports is expected to continue at the same rate as from Jan to Jun, what is the estimated number of exports in December 1999?	Answer: **B**

Working & Answer:

Rate of increase = (136.9 – 116.9) / 116.9 = 17.1086398%

Estimated exports in Dec 1999 = 136.9 x (1.171) = 160.32

Answer

160.3 (B)

Question 16: Which of the following results in the largest ratio?	Answer: **C**

Working & Answer:

A. "Exports in March to Imports in March"

116.7 : 108.9 = 1.0716

B. *"Imports in Jan, Feb and March to Imports in Apr, May and Jun"*

   110.0 + 112.4 + 108.9 = 331.3

   114.6 + 116.7 + 115.9 = 347.2

   331.3 : 347.2 = 0.9542

C. *"Exports to Imports in June"*

   136.9 : 115.9 = 1.1811

D. *"Imports to Exports in Feb"*

   112.4 : 117.8 = 0.9541

E. *"Total Imports to total Exports in Mar to Jun"*

   Total imports = 108.9 + 114.6 + 116.7 + 115.9 = 456.1

   Total exports = 116.7 + 124.9 + 128.8 + 136.9 = 507.3

   456.1 : 507.3 = 0.899

<u>Answer</u>

Exports to Imports in June (C)

Question 17: If a trader purchased 650 ounces of gold in 2000 and sold them all in 2005, how much money would they have made?	Answer: **A**

Working & Answer:

Cost of gold in 2000 : 650 ounces x $273 = $177,450

Sale price in 2005 : 650 ounces x $515 = $334,750

Therefore profit = $334,750 - $177,450 = $157,300

<u>Answer</u>

$157,300 (A)

Question 18: If a UK trader purchased 315 ounces of gold in 2005 when the exchange rate was £1:$1.6 and sold all of them in 2008 when the exchange rate had fallen to £1:$1.45, how much money did the trader make?	Answer: **D**

Working & Answer:

Cost of gold in USD in 2005 : 315 ounces x $515 = $162,225

At £1:$1.6, cost of gold in GBP = $\frac{\$162{,}225}{1.6}$ = £101,391

Sale price of gold in 2008 : 315 ounces x $865 = $272,475

At £1:$1.45, sale price of gold in GBP = $\frac{$272,475}{1.45}$ *= £187,914*

Thefefore profit in GBP = £187,914 - £101,391 = £86,523

Answer

£86,523 (D)

Question 19: *If a UK trader purchased 50 ounces of gold in 2001 when the exchange rate was $1:£0.67 and sold 1134 grams in 2007 when $1:£0.74, how much profit would they have made on the gold they sold? (1 ounce =28.35 grams)* — **Answer: A**

Working & Answer:

Sale price of gold in 2007 : $\frac{1134 \text{ grams}}{28.35}$ *= 40 ounces*

40 ounces x $835 = $33,400

At $1:£0.74, sale price of gold in GBP = $\frac{$33,400 \times 0.74}{1.45}$ *= £24,716*

Cost of gold in USD in 2001 : 40 ounces x $277 = $11,080

At $1:£0.67, cost of gold in GBP = $11,080 x 0.67 = £7,424

Therefore profit in GBP = £24,716 - £7,424 = £17,292

Answer

£17,292 (A)

Question 20: *Gold is expected to continue to increase over the next 2 years at the rate seen back in 2002-2004. If this happened what would the price of gold be at the end of 2011?* — **Answer: A**

Working & Answer:

Price increase of gold between 2002-2004 = $\frac{437 - 346}{346}$ *= 26.3%*

Therefore expected price of gold in 2011 = 1170 x 1.263

= $1,477.71

Answer

$1,478 (A)

Question 21: In 2005, what percentage of the population was aged 51 and over?	Answer: **A**

Working & Answer:

Number of people aged 51 and over in 2005 = 29.4 + 17.3 = 46.7

Total population in 2005 = 12.6 + 15.4 + 11.9 + 29.4 + 17.3 = 86.6

Percentage of population aged 51 and over = $\frac{46.7}{86.6}$ = 0.53926

<u>Answer</u>

53.93% (A)

Question 22: In 2005, 46% of 17-33 year olds were employed. If 6.1 million of those are employed full time, assuming the remainder are working part time how many are employed part time?	Answer: **D**

Answer:

Number of 17-33 year olds in employment = 46% * 15.4m = 7.084m

If 6.1m of those are working full time then the number employed part time is:

= 7.084m - 6.1m = 984,000

<u>Answer</u>

984,000 (D)

Question 23: In 1990, how many people were aged between 17 and 50? (in millions)	Answer: **C**

Working & Answer:

People aged between 17 and 50 in 1990 = 14.4 + 11.6 = 26.0

<u>Answer</u>

26.0 (C)

Question 24: Between which 5 years was the largest percentage change in the number of people aged 16 and younger?	Answer: **B**

Working & Answer:

1990 and 1995 = (13.2 - 12.1) / 12.1 = 9.09%

1995 and 2000 = (12.5 - 13.2) / 13.2 = (5.30%)

2000 and 2005 = (12.6 - 12.5) / 12.5 = 0.80%

<u>Answer</u>

1990 and 1995 (B)

Pyschometric Tests

Numerical

Test 3 answers

Question 1: In Month 5 and 6, part of the white bread mixture became contaminated resulting in below quality bread. This resulted in Fred's Bakery having to offer refunds plus a small compensation of £5 per loaf to each customer. 45% of white bread sold in Month 6 and 24% in Month 5 required a full refund to be paid to customers. If a white loaf of bread is sold for 80p per loaf, how much money has this cost Fred's Bakery?	Answer: D

Working & Answer:

Refund in Month 5 = 24% x 1,510 = 362.4 loaves
 = 362.4 x £0.80 = £289.92
 = £289.92 + (362.4 x £5 compensation)
 = £2,101.92

Refund in Month 6 = 45% x 1,490 = 670.5 loaves
 = 670.5 x £0.80 = £536.40
 = £536.40 + (670.5 x £5 compensation)
 = £3,888.90

Total cost to Fred's Bakery = £2,101.92 + £3,888.90
 = £5,990.82

<u>Answer</u>

£5,991 (D)

Question 2: Between which two months did brown bread and rolls/other see the largest percentage change in sales?	Answer: C

Working & Answer:

Months 1 - 2 = (940 + 390) − (790 + 412) = 10.65%
 (790 + 412)

Months 2 - 3 = (820 + 364) − (940 + 390) = (10.98%)
 (940 + 390)

Months 3 - 4 = (1,120 + 496) − (820 + 364) = 36.49%
 (820 + 364)

Months 4 - 5 = (976 + 841) − (1,120 + 496) = 12.44%
 (1,120 + 496)

Months 5 - 6 = (1,004 + 691) − (976 + 841) = (6.71%)
 (976 + 841)

<u>Answer</u>

Months 3 - 4 (C)

Question 3: What is the approximate proportion of brown bread sold in Month 3 and Month 5 to Total Sales?	Answer: E

Working & Answer:

Brown bread sold in Month 3 and Month 5 = 820 + 976 = 1,796

Total Sales in Month 3 and Month 5 = 2,153 + 3,327 = 5,480

Ratio = 1,796 : 5,480

The closest and best approximate ration is therefore 1:3

<u>Answer</u>

1:3 (E)

Question 4: If the cost of making one brown loaf is 10p more than a white loaf and if the total costs in Month 4 of making all white loaves was £483, what was the gross profit from brown bread in Month 4, assuming all loaves of bread are sold for 80p? (Gross profit is calculated as Sales less cost of sales)	Answer: C

Working & Answer:

Cost of making a white loaf in Month 4 = £483 / 1,150 = £0.42

Cost of making a brown loaf = £0.42 + £0.10 = £0.52

Gross profit of brown bread = 1,120 x (£0.80 - £0.52)

= £313.60

<u>Answer</u>

£313.60 (C)

Question 5: What is the difference in the average advertised price between 2004 and 2007?	Answer: C

Working & Answer:

Average advertised price in 2004 = £121,000 / 0.96 = £126,042

Average advertised price in 2007 = £180,000 / 0.985 = £182,741

Difference in price between 2004 and 2007 = £182,741 - £126,042 = £56,699

<u>Answer</u>

£56,699 (C)

Question 6: If in 2005 the average time a house was on the market was 29 days. How long did the average flat stay on the market in 2005?	Answer: C

Working & Answer:

Total proportion of time a house or flat was on the market = 3.2 x 34 days = 108.8 days

Total proportion of time a house was on the market = 2.2 x 29 days = 63.8 days

Average time a flat remained on the market in 2005 = 108.8 - 63.8 days = 45 days

<u>Answer</u>

45 days (C)

Question 7: If the average advertised price is expected to increase by 5% between 2007 and 2008, what is the percentage increase in the average selling price between the two years?	Answer: **E**

Answer:

The question provides enough information to calculate the listing price in 2008, however it is not possible to calculate the average selling price in 2008 as we are not informed of the average sale price as a percentage of advertised price figure. As such, this question cannot be answered.

Cannot Say (E)

Question 8: If the average selling price of a house in 2006 was £192,500, what was the average advertised price of a flat in 2006?	Answer: **A**

Working & Answer:

Total price of both houses and flats = £155,000 x 2.9 = £449,950

Amount relating to houses = £192,500 x 1.9 = £365,750

Therefore average selling price of flats in 2006 = £449,950 - £365,750 = £83,750

Average advertised price of a flat in 2006 = £83,750 / 0.97 = £86,340

<u>Answer</u>

£86,340 (A)

Question 9: How many more customers would company B require to generate the same turnover as that of A? (to the nearest million customers)?	Answer: **A**

Working & Answer:

Company A's turnover = 45% x £1,560m = £702m

Company B's turnover = 13% x £1,560m = £202.8m

Company B's number of customers = 13% x 86m = 11.18m

B's average turnover per customer = $\underline{£202.8m}$ = £18.1395349
                                      11.18m

In order for B to generate the same turnover of A an additional £499.2m (£702m - £202.8m) of turnover will need to be generated.

Therefore, the increase in customers for B would be = $\underline{£499.2m}$
                                                        18.1395349

= £27.52m

<u>Answer</u>

28 (A)

| Question 10: If A were to shut all its stores such that the customers went to stores D and E at a ratio of 6:5 how much money would D receive on the assumption that the new customers spend on average the same as the existing customers at D? | Answer: **B** |

Working & Answer:

Company D's turnover = 15% x £1,560m = £234m

Company D's number of customers = 20% x 86m = 17.2m

D's average turnover per customer = £234m / 17.2m = £13.6046512

Company A's number of customers = 30% x 86m = 25.8m

Number of A's customers to start using company B = 25.8m x 6/11 = 14.072727m

Therefore, the increase in turnover for D would be = 14.072727m x £13.6046512

= £191.4545m

Answer

£191m (B)

| Question 11: If the average spend of customers at C were to increase by £5.60, what level of turnover could Company C expect? | Answer: **D** |

Working & Answer:

Company C's turnover = 17% x £1,560m = £265.2m

Company C's number of customers = 12% x 86m = 10.32m

C's average turnover per customer = £265.2m / 10.32m = £25.70

Therefore, if the average spend of each customer increased by £5.60, the average customer would spend £31.30 (£25.70 + £5.60)

This would mean that Company C's total turnover would be = £31.30 x 10.32m

= £323.02

Answer

£323m (D)

| Question 12: Which store has the highest average spend per customer? | Answer: **A** |

Working & Answer:

Company A's turnover = 45% x £1,560m = £702m
Company A's number of customers = 30% x 86m = 25.8m
A's average turnover per customer = £702m / 25.8m = £27.210

Company B's turnover = 13% x £1,560m = £202.8m
Company B's number of customers = 13% x 86m = 11.18m
B's average turnover per customer = £202.8m / 11.18m = £18.140

Company C's turnover = 17% x £1,560m = £265.2m
Company C's number of customers = 12% x 86m = 10.32m
C's average turnover per customer = £265.2m / 10.32m = £25.70

Company D's turnover = 15% x £1,560m = £234m
Company D's number of customers = 20% x 86m = 17.2m
D's average turnover per customer = £234m / 17.2m = £13.6041

Company E's turnover = 10% x £1,560m = £156m
Company E's number of customers = 25% x 86m = 21.5m
E's average turnover per customer = £156m / 21.5m = £7.256

Answer

£27.21 - Store A (A)

Question 13: If the CO_2 emissions worldwide in 2005 were 1.6 billion, what was Germany's contribution to the 2007 CO_2 emissions if total emissions increased by 4% p.a. between 2005 and 2007? (to the nearest million) — **Answer: B**

Working & Answer:

Total emissions in 2007 = 1.6 billion x 1.04^2 = 1.73056 billion

Therefore Germany's contribution = 1.73056 billion x 8%

= 0.1384448 billion

Answer

138 million (B)

Question 14: Between the years 2005 to 2007 inclusive, which country had the largest CO_2 emissions? — **Answer: A**

Working & Answer:

Russia = 20 + 19 + 14 = 53

Germany = 11 + 9 + 8 = 28

UK = 9 + 7 + 9 = 25

USA = 34 + 33 + 21 = 88

China = 20 + 21 + 24 = 65

Answer

USA (A)

Question 15: It is expected that global CO2 emissions will decrease by 6.4% by 2010, however due to the increased production in China, it is also expected that China will increase it's CO2 emissions by 4.6% by 2010. What amount of CO2 emissions will the UK have in 2010? (2005 global emissions were 1.6bn)	Answer: **E**

Answer:

Although the question provides a lot of information in which to calculate an answer, the percentage proportion of CO2 emissions split by country in 2010 is not provided and hence this question cannot be answered.

Cannot Say (E)

Question 16: Within the UK, factories and offices contribute 68% of the CO2 emissions, cars 27%, houses 4%, and other 1%. If government regulations came into force such that UK factories and offices must cut their emissions by 20% and houses by 2%, with other sources remaining the same what will be the percentage of the emissions of the UK compared with the rest of the world based on 2007 data?	Answer: **D**

Working & Answer:

Percentage of factory emissions after government legislation = 68% x 0.8 = 54.4%

Percentage of house emissions after government legislation = 4% x 0.98 = 3.92%

Plus all other sources = 54.4% + 3.92% + 28% = 86.32%

Percentage of UK emissions compared to the rest of the world = 9% x 86.32%

= 7.7688%

<u>Answer</u>

7.8% (D)

Question 17: Which car manufacturer had the largest percentage of cars unsold in 2007?	Answer: **B**

Working & Answer:

FAIT = 1 - (1,273,000 / 1,872,000) = 32.0%

FORDS = 1 - (2,019,000 / 3,468,000) = 41.78%

CHEETAH = 1 - (827,000 / 1,118,000) = 26.03%

SAB = 1 - (599,000 / 982,000) = 39.0%

<u>Answer</u>

FORDS (B)

Question 18: CHEETAH's range of cars include the A1, A2, A3, A4 and A5. The A1 accounted for 19% of cars produced by CHEETAH, A2 for 19%, A3 for 26%, A4 for 12% and the A5 for the remaining. If out of the total A5's produced 86% were purchased by customers, how many A5's were sold in 2007? (in thousands)	Answer: **B**

Working & Answer:

Number of A5's produced = 100% - 19% - 19% - 26% - 12% = 24%
= 24% x 1,118 = 268.32

Number of A5's purchased = 268.32 x 86% = 230.7552

Answer

230.76 (B)

Question 19: FORDS and FAIT target the same customer base along with 7 other car manufacturers around the world. The total number of cars sold to this customer base in 2007 was 11.197 million, which is expected to grow by 4% p.a. for the next 7 years. FORDS aims to occupy 44% of this market by 2010. If so, how many more cars on average each year does FORDS need to sell in order to hit this target assuming the production growth will be the same each year for FORDS?	Answer: **D**

Working & Answer:

Total number of cars produced in 2010 = 11.197 million x (1.04^3) = 12.595 million

44% of this market is = 12.595 million x 0.44 = 5.541845 million

Ford currently sell 2.019m cars and will need to produce a further 3.5228 million (5.5418 – 2.019) a year by 2010.

Therefore increase in annual revenue necessary = 3.5228 million / 3 years = 1.17 million

Answer

1.17 million (D)

Question 20: SAB are planning on introducing a new model in 2008 which would increase it's production of all cars to 1.692m. If production of their current models are expected to increase by 4.2% in 2008, how many new model cars will need to be produced in 2008? (to the nearest thousand)	Answer: **D**

Working & Answer:

Total production of current car range in 2008 = 982,000 * 1.042 = 1.023 million

Therefore production of new model in 2008 = 1.692m – 1.023m = 668,756

Answer

668,756 (D)

Question 21: If in 1990, Mr Smith bought a house for €34,500, how much would the house be worth in 2000?	Answer: **E**

Answer:

The information in the graph provides the average house prices and hence it is not possible to answer what the actual house which Mr Smith bought in 1990 is worth in 2000.

Cannot Say (E)

Question 22: Between which 10 years did the housing market in the Poland perform the best? (at current prices)	Answer: C

Working & Answer:

1980 - 1990 = 28 – 17 = 11

1988 - 1998 = 66 – 26 = 40

1994 - 2004 = 110 – 22 = 88

1976 - 1986 = 24 – 14 = 10

<u>Answer</u>

1994 - 2004 (C)

Question 23: Mr Smith sold his house in 1992 for the average house price (current prices) and invested the full sale proceeds in a 3% p.a. fixed rate bond. If in 2002 Mr Smith wanted to get back onto the housing market at the average house price, how much additional money would he need to raise in order to afford this? (to the nearest thousand)	Answer: C

Working & Answer:

1992 average house price per graph = €30,000

If Mr Smith invests this amount in a fxied rate bond for 10 years:

€30,000 x 1.03^10 = €40,317

Average house purchase price in 2002 per graph = €90,000

Therefore additional finance required = €90,000 - €40,317

= €49,683

<u>Answer</u>

€50,000 (C)

Question 24: If in 1972 a house was purchased for 42% more than the average house price, in which of the following years would that person first see a return on their investment based on average current house prices?	Answer: C

Working & Answer:

Purchase price of house in 1972 =12 * 1.42 = €17.04

House price in 1974 = €13

House price in 1980 = €17

House price in 1984 = €22

House price in 1990 = €28

<u>Answer</u>

1984 (C)